A Millennial's Guide to Success and Employment

I0481294

By Alan H. Moore

Dedicated to my wife, Aini, and my two sons, Adam and Haris

Edited by Petrana Radulovic

Table of Contents

Introduction

As the Chief of Operations of a 401k administration company in Boca Raton, Florida for the past twenty-two years, I have learned something about millennials, since they are participants in the 5,000 company retirement plans that the company manages. At 17%, millennials are the largest population segment, which is projected to rise to 21% within five years; therefore, businesses are targeting them, hoping to capture a larger market share. In addition to the economic impact they are making, the social and political structure of the country is changing according to the interests and habits of millennials.

On the other hand, they are the first generation to be raised on cell phones, and are socially connected and over-praised by their parents to point of being unable to deal with failure and hardship like generations before. They don't trust government, institutions or brands, but they trust their Facebook "friends," and experiences posted on the web. Life, however, is too important to only live in the moment; it takes knowledge and skill to navigate the options available to young people looking for success today.

Therefore, I have put together some of my daily emails that I have sent to my blog of friends over the last fifteen years, which touch on the important things that millennials should know to be successful. In addition, employers should learn how to hire and deal with the workforce of the future. This book is a guide for both.

Prologue

I am often asked by graduates for pointers on interviewing and I tell them they need to communicate passion and confidence. The best interview I ever sat in was with a young man fresh out of college who said this, when I asked: "Tell me why I should hire you?"

He replied: "I just graduated with a Finance degree, but I don't know squat about your business. I owe 50k on a student loan and my parents are not well-off and I had to work my way through college. I don't care what you pay me, or what job you want me to do—I will learn anything you have to teach me and do any kind of work, any time of the day or night. I just want to work. I have to work and I need this job. Just give me a chance and you won't be sorry."

I hired him and was never sorry.

According to the *Sun-Sentinel* (2-5-17, p. 5D), management is not communicating effectively with employees. Instead, they deliver the company's myopic point of view while failing to listen to employee feedback, labeling it as complaining and ingratitude. The article urges employers to react better to employees that give suggestions on how to prevent problems before they occur, and not come down on them when a mistake is made. Even worse are the micro-managers who are often skeptical of the team's ability to work effectively, instead of trusting them to learn from their mistakes and improve operations. Communication is a two-way street and best served by clear, brief sentences punctuated with unambiguous details. After all, mission statements are mostly plagiarized, and speeches are a way to pave a one-way street.

On the other hand, it was Glasnost which brought down the Berlin Wall. It is a phrase that means increased "openness and transparency" in Russian and is an effective means to resolve conflict in organizations, but it is rarely used because management doesn't take criticism well—if used, though, Glasnost can take down that wall too.

Ray Dalio, CEO of the biggest hedge fund in the world, wrote a book entitled *Principles*, in which he explains the concept of "radical transparency," utilized in his company to harness conflict in order to achieve a "believable solution" that is derived by a consensus of peers. The point is, autocratic business decisions no longer work in a technically complicated environment; it takes a number of informed opinions analyzing problems at different angles to choose the right course: only an arrogant leader shuns the consensus and dictates the decision. Dalio's principle is to let the truth come out without repercussion—criticism and all—even if a billionaire like him has to eat crow. Because the objective is to win, to make the company grow profitably; and the best way to do that is to let consensus lead the way. If a CEO thinks he/she is the smartest guy in the room, then he/she didn't hire right. Therefore, it doesn't make sense to suppress dissent from workers if you hired right and want the truth. That's what Glasnost is all about, a search for the best truth, and it doesn't come easy; it takes conflict, which is healthy and not a sign of dysfunction.

In the future, there will be less tension and management will get easier, as computers will monitor robots, not people. In the meantime, conflict is what separates us from the robots and Glasnost is the algorithm.

Traditionally, every year employees will be reviewed by their boss who uses a checklist to score performance and deficiencies; that review determines a raise or not. It is often a one-sided, subjective meeting that is not helpful. There are two different mental states that exist in the room: the boss is focused on where performance needs to be improved, whereas, the employee wants to focus on compensation, job progression and career advancement. The boss dominates the conversation and the employee is too intimidated to speak his/her mind. Therefore, the discussion accomplishes very little and creates tension: if the employee objects to the boss's assessment, he risks being labeled defensive and a complainer. Often, the reviewer is influenced by feedback from others, who are biased and jockeying for the boss's attention themselves. The absurdity of the annual review is that the boss is rarely objective; he can't be without a personal one-on-one relationship with the employee.

The "Team" is spun by management as the most important thing, but good management is understanding each member of the team and their capabilities. That understanding creates a personal relationship and trust. To wit, the manager should strive to field the best team, and performance reviews should be focused on what functions the employee does and how effective they are, function by function. There is no overall performance rating that is meaningful, and pay is rarely dependent on performance...the truth is, pay is dependent on market forces and jobs have a pay range and a budget. At the end of a review, the boss will say something like: "You did a great job and I'm giving you a 3% raise which is twice the national average, congratulations." What's really being measured objectively in a review? Does pay really correlate with efficiency? I don't think so.

This is an example of the importance for a personal relationship between the boss and the employee when doing a review: the boss cites a subordinate's missing a high-profile meeting as cause for a reduced rating. What if the reason was something personal—perhaps a son picked up by the police—that the employee doesn't want to reveal? Why not reveal it? Because one-way accountability inevitably creates distrust. Does the boss self-reflect and ask, "What did I do, or should I be doing, to build trust?" Instead, the boss faults the employee for secretiveness. It's a vicious cycle.

Why wait a year to discuss with employees their performance? It should be an everyday, open-door, two-way relationship in order to develop a dynamic organization that is responsive to clients and to company goals. It shouldn't be a matter of getting the boss's ear and snagging a good performance rating.

Resolving conflicts with Glasnost and consensus building is the fundamental process of negotiating. For example, the oldest negotiated treaty on record between two independent nations is the Hittite-Egyptian deal done 3,000 years ago after both sides fought to a stalemate in the Battle of Kadesh in Syria. Both nations wanted to annex Syria and had a war over it for 80 years prior to the peace agreement forged in 1276 BC. The deal included some basic elements: there would be peace forever, border control, an exchange of prisoners and aid if either nation was attacked by another nation. It took 15 years to negotiate and neither emperor ever met the other; far humbler intermediaries did the whole thing.

A Harvard professor named Deepak Malhotra wrote a book about conflict titled *Negotiating the Impossible* and made some interesting observations that can be used today; the most important of which is ability to put yourself in the other guy's shoes— commonly known as empathy, the opposite of egotism. Deepak surmised that a successful agreement, either in Syria back then or in business today, must result in both sides being able to declare victory. That seems like an impossible conclusion when the conventional wisdom is that a deal is a zero-sum game where somebody must win and somebody must lose.

However, in business, when dealing seems hopeless, with offers being rejected over and over and participants have little power to force a conclusion, there needs to be a different approach—one that points out the value of doing business together, not the cost. Deepak postulates: "Impossible deadlocks and conflicts can be resolved if we shed the assumption that our only sources of leverage are money and power." It is not all about price; there can be no deal that lasts without trust...and that's why Glasnost is absolutely necessary. If you don't lay your cards on the table and tell the truth, you are not going to be trusted. Really, who trusts a sales pitch anymore? Less power point and more straight talk is what clients want.

Leadership

Colin Powell was interviewed in 2017 on TV by David Rubenstein and was asked what makes a great leader. Powell replied: "A leader sets the vision and defines the mission and then takes the message down to the lowest soldiers, or employees of an organization, explaining the value and purpose of the mission, in order to inspire them. He motivates and is never negative, and he gives the troops the tools they need to accomplish the task, letting them make the decisions in the field. A great leader is not an autocrat but a consensus builder and trusts his men as they must trust him not to send them on a bad mission and risk their lives needlessly."

That statement is counter intuitive to what most people think a leader or general should be like. However, to drive home his point, Powell told a story about Lincoln in the Civil War, when Lincoln got a telegram telling him that the Confederates had taken a Union outpost and captured 100 horses and a general.

Lincoln remarked to the messenger: "I sure hate to lose 100 horses."

The messenger asked: "What about the general?"

Lincoln replied: "I can make a general in five minutes, but 100 horses are hard to replace."

The point Lincoln and Powell were making is that a leader takes care of the "horses"—the men, employees, first, and gives them whatever they need to be successful, because they are the ones that win the war, not the generals. Powell kept a plaque on his desk at the Joint Chiefs with Lincoln's statement to remind him how unimportant he was—to keep his ego in check.

There was an article in *The Wall Street Journal* on 12-29-17, p. C2, about how the best leaders are captains on sports teams. And I quote: "...the greatest team captains were not gifted orators. They rarely formally addressed their teammates. They preferred to circulate widely, speaking to everyone in equal measure, always about the task at hand." I think this also defines bipartisanship.

The article referred to Jack Lambert of the Pittsburg Steelers, Bill Russell-Boston Celtics, Yogi Berra—NY Yankees, Vasilev of the Russian National Hockey Team.

These captains didn't hesitate to let the coaches know when they disagreed with them. They understood that conflict, when focused on supporting the team goals, is not destructive; it's essential to winning. Leaders are independent thinkers unafraid of dissent and what stands out about these leaders is that they were not great talents, nor charismatic—not the kind of people that give dazzling job interviews. They made their teams great by making the right choices on the job and under pressure, every hour, every day. It wasn't about personal glory; they worked for the greater good of the team and rarely uttered the word "I." The team members had 100% confidence in their captain and did what he said without question. They could win with him like no one else.

In 1980, the Russian hockey team was being ripped apart by their coach in the locker room for losing a game, when Vasilev, one of the veteran players, flew into a rage and grabbed the coach by the throat and threatened to kill him before he was calmed down by team members. Vasilev wasn't punished and neither men mentioned the incident in public. A month later the team elected Vasilev the captain, and the Kremlin and the coach let it stand. The Russian team became unstoppable winning three world championships—with their captain.

Now compare that leadership to what we have today. The President and the Republicans promise: "We are going to deliver jobs by giving rich people more money—because they are the job creators." Equally as bad for the country, the Democrats promise: "We are going to give more money to the poor and create equality for women." In other words, skip the jobs and make people more dependent on government.

To understand the leadership problem, the "Peter Principle" was created by a scholar of education named Laurence Peter about 60 years ago. The gist of his book was: "In a hierarchy, every employee tends to rise to his level of incompetence." The point is many managers strive to seem productive when in fact they're in over their heads and pass off pseudo-management wisdom for competence. Peter postulated that eventually a manager will get promoted to a "final level" because the people doing the appointing are incompetent as well. After all, when you're competent, even a dummy can see your output; and so, you are rewarded for that output. But once you have reached incompetence, there's little or no output from you. At this point, you are judged by your input— by how early you arrive at the office, how many meetings you attend and how cheerful you are, not to mention flattering the boss. Only "super-competence" will get you fired, because then you're making everyone else look bad; management simply can't recognize real efficiency. As Peter said, "the hierarchy must be protected at all costs".

Apply the Peter Principle to your career: try to avoid the "final level." In that endeavor, an employee can refuse promotions, but Peter said that causes too many problems. The best strategy is to master the art of "creative incompetence" and preemptively scuttle your chances for promotion by demonstrating incompetence at something irrelevant that won't get you fired but removes you from the short-list for upper management. Peter offered a few helpful suggestions, such as being marginally rude to the boss' spouse at the holiday party, dressing just slightly inappropriately, or getting a tattoo on the neck above the collar.

In Peter's final analysis, a business shouldn't try to fire all the incompetent managers because they would be replaced by deadwood anyway. Albeit, these incompetent people have families to feed, cars to buy and vacations to take and thus they are the real job-creators in a consumer driven economy. Peter argued that incompetent people will do the least damage to competent people's productivity if we maintain the benign illusion that they're useful and have a bright future. The only situation where that is not true is in Congress, where illusion drafts legislation and the real damage occurs.

As an example of preemptive incompetence, about 35 years ago, with my new finance degree, I was hired to be a loan officer at a bank in Roanoke, Virginia and I was given an office and a secretary with 20 years of experience, but I didn't know the first thing about making a real estate loan. On my first day a man came into the outer office, so I picked up the phone and started to pretend that I was working on a big loan, throwing large figures around so the guy could hear me, and made a big commitment before I waved him in and hung up.

"Can I help you?" I said.

He replied, "Yeah, I've come to activate your phone line."

Fortunately, only the secretary witnessed the event, and she just smiled and didn't tell anyone what a fool I was. However, she had "Peter Principle" written all over her face. She knew who belonged in that office and so did I.

Entrepreneurship

Entrepreneurship is a micro value and it is hard to teach: some people have it and some don't. They say America was built by entrepreneurs, even with the 90% failure rate that startup businesses face. You could also say this country was built on failure and that the freedom to fail is our real heritage. In that regard, failure is not so bad, but the failure to get up and try again is. Commitment is grounds for success, like a ham & eggs breakfast, the chicken was involved, but the pig was committed.

Take my uncle, Walter, for example. He grew up in the early 1900s and he told me a story in 1958 about when he was a boy trying to get ahead. Walter loved animals and raised hamsters as a hobby. He used to buy baby hamsters from a pet store in Richmond for fifty cents each; in turn, the store bought them from a producer for twenty-five cents. Walter figured out that he could buy pregnant hamsters from the store and sell back the babies and make a huge profit.

So, he went to the library and read all about it and even talked to a vet, who told him how to tell the difference between the pregnant ones and the not. He developed a keen eye for motherhood, because the store owner couldn't tell the difference. Carefully, he would pick up all the hamsters in the store and look at their bellies, and Walter could determine which ones were about to drop. Since there were ten in the average litter, he could make a profit of 400% in just several weeks (buy one at 50, sell back 10 at 25). It was an entrepreneur's dream, but it was real. The only thing that limited his revenue growth was the market for hamsters for that particular store; there were just so many hamsters the proprietor could sell. So, Walter went to other stores and was making more profit than any of the store owners by the time he was 15 years old. He had the knack, but most want-a-preneurs don't; that's why the failure rate is so high.

All too often, people go into business and fail, only to work for someone else for less money than they could have made if they had succeeded. But that's fair and it's efficient, as long as the government doesn't bail out the failures, which is what happened in the crisis of 2008. With every subsidy and tax break, somebody is being bailed out. Every one of us is "entitled" to fail or succeed, but that doesn't mean being able to pass on huge estates, while so many don't have a quality education necessary to prepare for the entrepreneurship gamble. Forced or otherwise, excess capital must be reinvested in the socio-economic structure to maintain efficient markets. That's not socialism; it is pragmatic capitalism. Uncle Walter used to say: "After you buy everything you need, everything else is just showing off." I continue to practice what Walter preached and hope my millennials will get the message. America needs more entrepreneurs.

Productivity

Profits of corporations fall as productivity falls, which is simply a calculation of how many labor dollars it takes to produce a widget. A decline in productivity can happen in two ways: either you need more people to produce the same amount of goods and services or you must pay the same amount of people more money because of a skilled labor shortage. But either way the corporation does worse, unless of course production is expanding because of new demand. Automation is the wave of the future: replacing people with robots that don't get a paycheck. In the past, companies outsourced jobs to become more productive, but that trend is ending as Artificial Intelligence develops.

A *Wall Street Journal* (1-13-18, p. C1) article delved into the question: "What determines performance the most: talent or working harder and more hours?" The answer: neither. Top performers master selectivity and are able to prioritize which tasks to take on. They focus exclusively on the few important ones. People that can apply intense, targeted effort on priorities are the most productive. Talent, effort and luck matter as well, but not as much.

In other words, individual productivity requires using the fewest steps in a process, attending the fewest meetings, setting the fewest goals and measuring progress with the fewest metrics. You should un-confuse and unravel the whirlwind of activity that surrounds you and put your blinders on. Also important is the ability to say "no" to bad ideas and to unproductive tasks that are dumped on you.

The author of the article cited her experience in doing a proposal for a CEO of a large company. Just before she began her presentation, the CEO said that he only wanted to see one slide, when she had prepared 15. On the fly, she thought: "one slide; what is the key issue here?" Then she selected one and it worked. She looked back on the situation and reflected: "Since I didn't take the time to present 15 slides, the CEO and I were able to spend 45 minutes discussing the program in greater depth. At the end, he remarked how productive the meeting was."

To be productive you must get rid of the clutter and concentrate on what's important. Data shows that working 50 hours a week is about all you need to be the most productive, if you learn to focus and stay off the iPhone. Just remember, when presenting your message to others, one slide will do—if you select the right one; 15 becomes a confusing distraction that often misses the point. To make a sale, you must get to the point in order to win your point; so, skip the long boring story about how you thought of it.

The concern for employees: does better work lead to better pay? The answer: not in most companies. One reason is because workers aren't allowed to share pay information; such sharing is a cardinal sin to management. According to a study by Cornell University, performance is hindered by not linking better work to better pay. Some companies, like Whole Foods, have already caught on, making salaries more transparent to reduce the resentment that comes with discovering a co-worker's higher pay and to prove that no gender gap exists in the organization. Nationally, women are paid 80.5% of what men are in the same position and it's a problem. Legally, employers aren't allowed to retaliate against workers for discussing their pay, though that can be hard to enforce if an employer is an at-will state and doesn't say why an employee is being fired. The old school of thought on the issue is to keep everyone's pay secret, which primarily benefits the employer, because pay can't be compared against performance at the employee level and used to negotiate a higher salary.

In any case, through Glass Door and published industry comparisons on the internet, workers can discover their fair market value and take that information into their annual reviews. Albeit, the efficient employer, who can produce more work per worker than the competition, can afford to pay higher wages and attract the best talent and should do so. The more that employees realize that their jobs are paying above market, the better off the employer is. However, that is counterintuitive to an employer. Nevertheless, transparency works better than keeping secrets; not only does it build trust, but it makes performance and profit the goals workers strive for—believing that they will share. If you build a meritocracy, workers will go for it and the company will thrive. Otherwise "efficiency and growth" are viewed as empty words from management to justify anemic pay raises.

As connected as millennials are, do you really think workers believe that tax cuts and more growth will lead to higher pay? Corporate profit margins were at an all-time high in 2017 and wages only increased 2.4% on average. Instead of believing the spin, employees will leverage the current shortage of skilled labor to extract higher raises in 2018. The biggest complaint employers have today is that they can't find enough workers; but that's because existing pay rates are too low and most skilled laborers already have a job. The bottom line for business owners: pay your workers more or lose your best ones to a competitor, and efficiency-wise, it wouldn't hurt to be more transparent about it. Taking subjectivity out of annual reviews would also go a long way to increasing productivity, which is not all about investing more in technology and robots; it's about motivating people to work smarter, tying pay to production and profits.

MarketWatch, December 2017 posed this question: What are the biggest distractions at work?

Psychologist Larry Rosen wrote: "Technology, particularly cell phones, are the No. 1 distraction in almost all studies — it's the one that creates the interruptions. About half of interruptions we get are from the outside, most often an email or text message. The other half of the interruptions come from inside our brain. They are often caused because we are feeling a need to stay constantly connected so we need to check in often. We know that people check in every 15 minutes or less and, as soon as they check in it will take upwards of 20 minutes to return to the task they were working on. It doesn't mean the work is not productive, but if you stop what you're working on immediately and come back to it 20 minutes later you have to activate all the areas you were using. That project is now going to take you longer to finish, and because you are constantly interrupted, there will be more stress and anxiety involved."

As employees everywhere keep their cell phones out of sight at their desks, responding to every text on the sly, businesses have a problem: a loss of productivity. How do managers manage that problem if they are getting just as many text messages as everyone else? The answer is to turn the cell phones off at work. I often get laughed at because I keep my flip-phone in the car for emergencies and don't text. But, then, I stay on top of my work. I can remember the old days when the company policy was to not allow personal phone calls, but technology has changed all that. It's hard to stop texting once you are addicted to it, but there are more productive things to do and not enough time to do them if you check in every 15 minutes. So, stop checking.

Even though managing phone-time represents a personal challenge for workers, there can be no doubt of the efficiencies derived from new technologies, such as faster-smaller-cheaper computers and chips; the internet and apps; and the use of robots to replace humans. For example, it now takes 12 employees, on average, working at a McDonalds to handle the busy lunch hour; twenty years ago, it took 25. Automation brings efficiency.

After the war in 1945, America possessed 50% of the earth's manufacturing capacity, two thirds of the gold reserves and produced more oil than the rest of the world combined. That's because Japan and Europe were decimated and couldn't compete, and China was a million rice paddies connected by rickshaw with no factories. Since then, global competition has created the capacity to over-produce everything, yet the vast wealth created after the war still remains, looking for a return other than from capital investment, which was the mother of employment in the past. The old way of doing business is gone: i.e., the division of duties and breaking down production into rote operations for efficiency. The new manager is software, hosted by micro computer power. An algorithm can do anything a human brain can do; therefore, a business needs fewer managers and more automation—which produces a flat management structure instead of the typical pyramid. After all, a robot doesn't get a salary— and a robot needs a maintenance man not a manger.

Efficiency requires less management and more workers that know how to operate the "program," because software and the "big data" that it creates knows and stores everything that happens in real-time; all you must do is fetch it with SQL. The bottom line: 1) workers need to be tech-trained to be employed in the future and make a decent wage and 2) businesses will merge departments to reduce management personnel and cut costs in the attempt to flatten the structure. If they don't do it, the competition will flatten them.

Therefore, software is the answer to cost efficiency in this extremely competitive environment. Times may be different, but the goal is the same: to make money and to do that, you need skilled workers that can program, or at least operate one. That starts with education. To give you an idea how education is going, here is a grade-school math question morphing over the decades:

Math in 1950: A logger sells a truckload of lumber for $100. His cost of production is 4/5ths of the price. What is his profit?

Math in 1960: A logger sells a truckload of lumber for $100. His cost of production is 4/5ths of the price, or $80. What is his profit?

Math in 1970: A logger exchanges a set "L" of lumber for a set of "M" of money. The cardinality of set "M" is 100: What is the cardinality of the set "P" of profits?

Math in 1980: A logger sells a truckload of lumber for

31

$100. His cost of production is $80 and his profit is $20. Your assignment: Underline the number 20.

By 1990, logging and math took a serious hit: By cutting down beautiful forest trees, the logger makes $20. What do you think of this way of making a living? Topic for class participation after answering the question: How did the forest birds and squirrels feel as the logger cut down the trees? (There are no wrong answers).

By 2000, basic math was kidnapped by public accounting and buried in footnotes: A logger sells a truckload of lumber for $100. His cost of production is $120. How does Goldman Sachs determine that his profit margin is $60?

In 2008, the lack of applied math crashed the housing market and entire economy, which is now a footnote in most financial statements.

In 2016, math is back in vogue and hiding in algorithms—and only high SAT scores know enough math: that's why all the top companies only hire 3.5

GPAs or higher—Goldman Sachs doesn't interview less than a 3.8.

The moral is: as corporate structure flattens, the people remaining at the top must be smarter than a robot and that's hard to do if you don't know basic math and are not software aware.

Success and Happiness

As my Uncle Walter used to say: "Success is getting what you want and happiness is wanting what you get." He told me that on my eleventh birthday when he handed me a present. It was a pencil.

"What's that for?" I asked.

"So, you can write your goals down. Make two columns and head them Success and Happiness and then list your top three things in each."

So, I did. For success I wrote: lots of money, to be a quarterback, and to own a race car. For happiness I listed: get a dog, meet Gene Autry, and go to Disneyland.

Two weeks later, I'm sitting in my 5th grade Geography class looking out the window, wishing the bell would ring, when I saw Uncle Walter drive up in his Edsel. He saw me in the window and honked just as the bell rang and I ran to the curb. On the front seat was a collie and Walter smiled and said: "His name is

Rebel; now get in, we're going to see Gene Autry. He's in a parade in Pasadena tomorrow and I have two plane tickets in my pocket. I already cleared it with your parents."

We dropped the dog off at home and flew to California where I not only got Gene Autry's autograph, but squeezed in a visit to Disneyland. When we got home, there was Rebel on the front porch and I never felt happier—Success has never come close to that day.

As I walked with Walter to his car he asked me, "What did you learn on the trip son?"

I answered: "That you can't buy happiness, like the minister always says."

Agitated, Walter shook his head: "Of course you can; all your happiness the past few days came from me, and I worked my tail off for the money it took... so study hard and become successful; and you can buy down your list yourself.

Eventually, you will find that success and happiness aren't things, they are a process. But, nobody under the age of 50 would know that. In the meantime, I'm only 82 and I've got to get back to my work—see you next birthday."

Walter's legacy lives on in me: You can buy happiness if you can pay the price.

Facebook and the iPhone have changed people's relationship with society and each other; both have been constructed to consume maximum time for users and to follow your every click. Swiping, scrolling, posting, and texting is the new passive way of life, replacing positive action and real reading. The root of success in anything is perseverance, which takes time and patience; and there is a growing attention deficit. In theory, technology is supposed to bring us products that save time; instead, it has brought us a time suck. Who really has time for hundreds of "friends" and all the posting, texting and following that they take? I had five friends growing up and that was too many to keep track of. Of course, friends back then would lend you money; today they will only lend you their time, as if time is as valuable as money—which it isn't when it's spent on Facebook. The one good thing posting has done is cause de-branding; people can quickly read about product quality and service from the user experiences on the web. Trip Advisor for example, where the best hotel is not determined by its brand anymore but by what people say. The same goes for Yelp.

Poet Dylan Thomas said: "There is only one thing that's worse than an unhappy childhood, and that's having a too happy childhood." Adversity causes stress. "Coping with stress is like exercise: we get stronger with practice." (*WSJ*, 11-11, p. C1)

Clinical psychologists found that the most important quality to possess to be successful is perseverance. Victor Goertzel studied thousands of famous and successful people and determined that 75% of them grew up in homes plagued by poverty, abuse, absent parents, alcoholism or some other misfortune. The ability to bounce back from a difficult childhood instills the confidence and determination necessary to overcome problems all through life. The most determined have the mindset: "I am a fighter—I will survive—I never lose hope." (WSJ IBID)

You can't learn that mindset with a perfect childhood; so be careful what you do for your children. If you want them to be successful and independent, love them the right way, which is not too much for too long.

There are many studies on the subject of money and happiness. A Harvard Business School professor, Mike Norton, did a study that determined that rich people getting even richer experienced zero gain in happiness. When asked what amount of additional money would make them happier, they all said two or three times what they had. At that stage of wealth, the rich said that only spending money on other people made them happy, not spending it on themselves, which defies the American dream that billionaires are happier than we are.

Norton's work indicates that the widening inequality gap in America is not a matter of simple justice and moral reckoning, but it is a threat to happiness on both sides of the gap. It's not just bad for the poor, but also for the rich also. If only Congress could use Norton to do tax reform, we could all be happier.

Abbott and Costello explored the depth of success and money and came up with an investment plan.

> Abbot: What are you doing with all your money? The market is looking risky here: North Korea, the PE of Dow is 24, everything is high.
>
> Costello: I already stashed it in a drain in my basement ten years ago.
>
> Abbott: How much do you have down there?
>
> Costello: About a million bucks.
>
> Abbott: Maybe you should invest it in the stock market and buy the dip when it comes. There is still a lot left in the bull.
>
> Costello: I did that in 2007 and lost half of it in the crash of 2009.
>
> Abbott: Are you nuts? Why did you sell? The market is way higher than the peak in 2007 and more than three times the low in 2009.

Costello: Because when it crashed, you said half a loaf is better than none, so I took the half that was left and put it down the drain.

Abbott: Well, now I think you should take the million and put it in the market and get a return like everybody else.

Costello: What! A return to 2009?

Abbott: No, a profit return, or dividend return— any return is better than throwing money down your drain.

Costello: No, it's not; every payday I put more money in the drain and my cash-stash always get bigger. I don't need a return to have more.

Abbott: I see your point, money down the drain is good if it's your drain...OMG, that's a new investment theory.

Costello: Well, it's my money, and the surest way to end up with million bucks in the stock market is to start with two million in a bull market. Been there and done that!! And now I'm sure about what I've got.

Abbott: You should write a book and call it "How to Get Rich Going Down the Drain".

Costello: You laugh, but my way is better than getting poor investing in a lot of bull.

Abbott: Well said, my boy. I may go down the drain with you.

The moral of the story is that saving your way to wealth is more certain than investing your way to wealth. As long as you have a paycheck and discretion over your spending, you can make it happen for sure.

Remember, it is your constitutional right to the "pursuit of happiness" and profit in the stock market. But, that doesn't mean you will find it.

The following, is one man's grave advice on the happiness issue:

Headstone of Russell J. Larsen in the Logan City Cemetery, Logan, Utah

FIVE RULES FOR MEN TO FOLLOW FOR A HAPPY LIFE:

1. It's important to have a woman who helps at home, cooks from time to time, cleans up, and has a job.

2. It's important to have a woman who can make you laugh.

3. It's important to have a woman who you can trust and doesn't lie to you.

4. It's important to have a woman who is good in bed and likes to be with you.

5. It's very, very important that these four women do not know each other, or you could end up dead like me.

In relationships and in business, conflicts continually arise. If you're not good at resolving conflicts, you will fail to solve problems effectively, and fail in your personal life too. Your happiness and your career are at stake. Starting with the mission statement of life, "the quest for happiness," what would happen if I asked my friends and business associates the question: "Are you happy?" According to a Harvard study, most of them would say: "Yes… Kinda… not really." Just "Kinda unhappy" and yet they are in the top one tenth of 1% of all the people on the earth as to opportunity and wealth. That's a depressing thought.

If one of them told any of the poverty-stricken people in India that they were unhappy, the Indian would say: "Are you crazy, what's your problem?" The problem can be broken down into two elements: circumstance and choices. The top 10% of incomes in America have the best circumstances in the world for their advantage, though they often make bad choices. However, the poor are plagued with bad circumstances, in addition to having no choice but to exist in poverty. Money could buy them happiness because they know how to appreciate it.

On an individual level, to resolve conflict you must have empathy for the other side and be able to put yourself in their shoes. Being able to resolve conflicts will make you happier and more successful. Empathy requires two things: humility and confidence. It takes both in equal doses. For example, when you approach a problem at work and say to yourself, "We can fix it, but I need help because I have my limitations," you are expressing both confidence and humility in recognizing that you need to work as a team to get the job done.

Too often, I conflict with people controlled by their ideology and arrogance, who start every other sentence with "I" and who are unable to listen and empathize with the other side. They are right and everyone that disagrees with them is wrong. However, the best ending to a negotiation or conflict is when the other side walks away saying: "I don't agree with you, but I was heard and my view was thoughtfully considered." Listening is the door to fairness.

97% of the US population worries most about not having enough money, while the top 3% don't appreciate having too much. Even the upper middle class has been split by the "Great Acceleration" in wealth over the past thirty years and that divergence will become more pronounced with the new tax bill. Those making huge salaries jealously watch the rich get richer because they own most of the capital. But, even the rich aren't happy, as they compete among themselves for status: who has the biggest mansion?

Will their kids get into Harvard or Stanford? All the while, their relationships suffocate from the drive to have more, even though the cost is too high: time.

For example, Fox's number one talk show host, Bill O'Reilly, was fired and other ones like him have fallen, leaving a grave yard of broken relationships. "Sic transit Gloria Mundi," or as Jack Dempsey use to say, "the bigger they are, the harder they fall." Even at a Pope's coronation, a monk says, "*Pater sancte, sic transit gloria mundi*," to remind the Pope that despite the grandeur of the office, he is a mortal man. Bill didn't think he was mortal and fell in infamy, despite having gone to Harvard. That's how it goes for a prime-time anchor with a high education when he can't keep his ego under control.

To wit, an American businessman was at the pier of a little coastal Mexican village when a small boat with just one fisherman docked in the early afternoon. Inside the small boat were several large tuna and the American then asked why he didn't stay out longer and catch more fish.

The Mexican said he had enough to support his family's immediate needs.

45

The American then asked, "But what do you do with the rest of your time?"

The Mexican fisherman said, "I sleep late, fish a little, play with my children, take siesta with my wife, and stroll into the village each evening where I sip wine and play guitar with my amigos. I have a full and busy life, señor."

The American scoffed, "I am a Harvard MBA and could help you. You should spend more time fishing and with the proceeds buy a bigger boat, with the proceeds from the bigger boat you could buy several boats, eventually you would have a fleet of fishing boats. Instead of selling your catch to a middleman you would sell directly to the processor, eventually opening your own cannery. You would control the product, processing and distribution. You would need to leave this small coastal fishing village and move to Mexico City, then LA and eventually NYC where you will run your expanding enterprise."

The Mexican fisherman asked, "But senor, how long will this all take?" To which the American replied, "15 or 20 years."

"But what then, señor?"

The American laughed and said, "That's the best part. When the time is right you would announce an IPO and sell your company stock to the public and become very rich, you would make millions."

"Millions, señor? Then what?"

The American said, "Then you would retire. Move to a small coastal village where you would sleep late, fish a little, play with your kids, take siesta with your wife, stroll to the village in the evenings where you could sip wine and play your guitar with your amigos."

The moral is: making money takes time, so be sure you really want the money that takes it. At some point, you must fish or cut bait, because time doesn't wait.

Understanding Millennials

Millennials' addiction to the iPhone is an epidemic. *MarketWatch* (5-19-17) reports "25% of millennials look at their phone more than 100 times a day compared with just 10% of baby boomers, according to a survey of 2,600 people across five countries conducted by mobile device care company B2X. Half of millennials look at their phone more than 50 times a day — three times the rate of boomers. One in four millennials spend five hours a day on their phones and 50% spend at least 3 hours."

I've never met a millennial not on food stamps that didn't have a cell phone and stared at it every ten minutes—no matter who they were with. If success is predicated on persistence and drive, the typical millennial doesn't have a chance. "Five hours a day" wasted on texting, with thumbs tapping like jack hammer. I don't own an iPhone and my kids would have to go into counseling if their phones got swiped— and the real-world experience is just a swipe away—I would hire a thief if it wasn't for the GPS in the phones.

Millennial phone addicts typically live with mom and dad and don't pay utilities; they are content to hang out with friends and swipe their lives away, all the while wondering how to pay back their student loans. In that context, "swipe" is a double entendre, both a source and cure for the addiction. But, a millennial wouldn't know what double entendre means—because few of them have read a book since "Catcher in the Rye" in the ninth grade. After all, texting "double entendre" has no abbreviation and takes too much thumbing.

Age 30 is hitting the downside of millennialism: the age when people often wonder where they stand in the race to success and material things. By 30, the average millennial should have saved a year's worth of salary to be on track with that peer group, according to Fidelity Investments. By age 35, twice the salary. However, the median retirement savings for a worker in their 30s was $45,000, according to Transamerica Center for Retirement Studies, which looked at workers' retirement accounts including employer contributions to 401k-s. (*MarketWatch* 5-22-17).

According to a Pew survey in November 2017, less than 10% of millennials can name one US Senator and half are not affiliated with any church or political party. Pew says millennials are "at or near the highest levels of political and religious disaffiliation recorded for any generation in the quarter-century." Despite the alienation from politics and churches and high levels of social distrust, they are arguably the most optimistic about America's future... "with a little help from their friends" (the Beatles), they can do anything.

However, millennials distrust government and think Social Security won't be there for them; and most disapprove of ObamaCare because they don't think they need insurance and don't want to carry it. They hated the $695 tax penalty for not being insured, before the Republicans repealed it in 2018. Otherwise, millennials are conventional when it comes to employment. A Manpower Group survey found that compensation influences their choice of employment the most, with a 53% importance level. 38% of workers say flexibility is second. Four out of five millennials said they would change jobs for the same pay for better training opportunities. They want to learn.

The bottom line: if you want to hire talent you must pay-up for it and offer a flexible work schedule and good training. Highly educated millennials also want their pay to reflect their impact on the organization's growth and profit, like stock options and performance bonuses—If they can't get ahead in one company they will jump to another, and in a tight labor market, they can jump.

Another intangible that influences younger workers comes from their past: they have grown up connected by social media and want to be heard and praised. They think the employer should appreciate them more than they should appreciate the job. After all, there are other jobs in a full-employment economy. An employer must bring down their expectations gently, but also realize that the old days are over, when the boss could bark out policy changes and expect the workforce to grin and bear it. Times have truly changed and disgruntled employees aren't shy about posting on Glassdoor and plastering management.

Living in the moment, financially grounded in the Bitcoin experience, selfie-ing this and that, texting until midnight—Millennials are said to be impatient, unfocused, entitled, lazy and unable to deal with failure and stress, satisfied with a venti latte in the morning, a studio apartment with Wi-Fi and net-zero in the bank after all the automatic debits have cleared— but, it's not their fault. It is caused by bad parenting.

These young people grew up being told they were special and could be anything they want— emotional stress never entered their environments. Their parents argued with teachers who didn't give them an A; they made sure medals and trophies were given to their super darlings for just showing up, for participating instead of winning in sports and other activities. The kids were praised for whatever they did and told how great they were when they weren't even close. Now they are grown and going to work and finding out they are not special, and that you get nothing for coming in last; that work is a necessity of life and not intended to be a titillating experience. In shock and frustration, they turn to their technology addiction, and to their Facebook/Instagram friends: routinely texting the same message to ten pseudo-friends—hi………. hi……..hi……—in an ego-numbing circle back to their adolescence obsession: the days when they were protected from the pain of losing, because their parents never allowed failure to be mentioned. It is a fact that smoking and alcohol addiction usually starts in adolescence, and the iPhone/social media connection is just as real.

No doubt, millennials lack the toughness to absorb hardship, pain and discipline. They say they are looking for "purpose" in a job, and the ability to make an "impact," but they don't have the upbringing to make it happen; and it's not their doing. Innocently, they believed their parents who lied to them, and are still lying to them by providing support long after they start working. The truth parents should be telling is, "live within your means—if you want more, work longer and harder. Failure is a consequence that you will have to face many times in your life and society doesn't owe you a thing." My message to millennials is this: "The best selfie is the one you didn't take, and never pick up an iPhone until after quitting time. You are not a kid anymore protected by your social network. It's just you and what you can do, but you need to have confidence in yourself. "

This is a story to drive that point home.

It's a story about a friend of Uncle Walter's who faced bankruptcy in the Depression and it tells what confidence can accomplish. The friend was a business owner who was deep in debt and could see no way out. Creditors were hounding him and suppliers had his company on COD. As he sat on a park bench in New York, head in hands, wondering if anything could save him, an old man suddenly appeared in front of him.

"I can see that something is troubling you," he said.

After listening to the executive's problem, the old man said, "I believe I can help you."

He asked the man his name, wrote out a check, and pushed it into his hand saying, "Take this money. Meet me here exactly one year from today, and you can pay me back at that time."

Then he turned and walked away as quickly as he had come. The business executive saw in his hand a check for $500,000, signed by John D. Rockefeller, the richest man in the world!

"I can erase my money worries in an instant!" he realized. But instead, the executive decided to put the uncashed check in his safe. Just knowing it was there might give him the strength to work out a way to save his business, he thought.

With renewed optimism, he negotiated better deals and extended terms of payment. He closed several big sales and within a few months he was out of debt and making money once again. Exactly one year later, he returned to the park with the uncashed check and at the agreed-upon time, the old man appeared. But just as the executive was about to hand back the check and share his success story, a nurse came running up and grabbed the old man.

"I'm so glad I caught him!" she said. "I hope he hasn't been bothering you. He's always escaping from the nursing home and telling people he's John D. Rockefeller." And she led the old man away by the arm.

The executive was stunned: all year long he'd been wheeling and dealing, buying and selling, convinced he had half a million dollars behind him. Suddenly, he realized that it wasn't the money, that had turned his life around; it was his newfound self-confidence that gave him the power to achieve anything he went after.

With confidence, the impact of the millennial generation on America will be profound, since it will rise to be 21% of the population within five years. We will be relying on these youngsters to join the work force and keep Social Security and Medicare solvent, to innovate the next generation of economic prosperity, and yet they must command enough resolve and determination to deal with the external threats that will face the country, like North Korea and Iran, and the internal ones too, like the national debt and income inequality, which will result in anarchy if it is not corrected. Ironically, the one thing they have going for them is their willingness to connect socially; they like all people in general and don't feel alienated from society or the rest of the globe. Their narcissism gives them the belief that they can do anything, and the world is their oyster. Hopefully, the work environment will teach them how to make pearls. Like all generations, they will learn to be productive Americans.

This is an email I received from a millennial with his head on straight. He is 23 and on my blog list.

[Tim]
Sent: Friday, December 01, 2017 9:52 AM
To: Alan Moore[alanm@slavic401k.com]
Subject: Re: Baking In tax Reform & Millennial Madness

"Hey Mr. Moore,

Given what I think may be a unique stance on this, I wanted to contribute to this ongoing discussion. Back in March at my company's South Florida managers meeting, we watched the Simon Sinek video on millennials in the workplace. We followed up with this video on how the environment in the electrical industry is changing. It was a great discussion, mostly led by the division manager and some of the more prominent managers in the division. Toward the end of the discussion, the manager that I am currently training under in Fort Myers said that he disagreed with what society has to say about millennials. He said they are intelligent, creative, and some of the hardest workers in his business. What I am sure he did not expect was for me to negate his response and defend the idea that millennials are lazy and entitled. Obviously as a member of the millennial generation, I have more face time with this population than those of other generations. What I have experienced on a large scale is that my peers believe they are over-worked and underpaid. They think that a full-time position means 40 hours a week, and $70,000 is a reasonable starting salary just because they have a degree. They see people that have been in the business for 20+ years and believe they deserve the same caliber of respect and pay. I concluded my response by saying all millennials will be lazy and entitled, until they are not. I was lazy and entitled until I was not.

I believe there is a tipping point in most of our lives where responsibility and gaining respect become a priority rather than instant gratification, but unfortunately for many millennials that tipping point appears to come too late (luckily for me, I believe it came when I worked my weekends as a dishwasher in high school). The upside is that some of these kids that think they are worth more than their $40,000 starting salary go on to be entrepreneurs, thinkers, and people that bring innovation to the world.

Here is my message to millennials: Take your lumps, the starting salary, and the 60-hour work week. Seek to earn the respect of those around you through character, diligence, and ethic. Set your goals high, and don't stop until you get there.

I will leave you with a saying my father has that has stuck with me through life and I continue to share with people questioning their professional position post-graduation - "Hard now, easy later. Easy now, hard later."

Tim paid his own way through college working 40 hours a week and shared a house with my son, so I got to know him well. I am certain that he is bound to succeed.

Having personally interviewed and hired over 1000 people in my career, I have an opinion on how recent graduates should seek employment. I advise them to skip boiler-plated rhetoric in their resume and keep it short and factual. Resume robots often use phrases like: "good at multitasking," "have strong interpersonal skills," "enjoy a challenge," "work hard to attain goals"—self-aggrandizing doesn't mean much to an interviewer, as he/she attempts to determine a candidate's character and capabilities in a brief encounter. I look for three things in an interview: can the kid learn what the company wants to teach them? Will he/she work hard and stick with a task until it is finished? And—can I trust them? (Often called integrity). Hiring someone is always an educated guess and the real mistake is not firing them quickly if you are wrong. That's what internal controls are all about: catching mistakes, human or otherwise.

Warren Buffet had this to say about who he hires and why:

Cynthia the interviewer: *"Our students are always interested in knowing what you look for when you hire someone? What specific qualities do you seek?"*
Warren: *"You look for three things, you look for intelligence, you look for energy and you look for integrity. You don't need to be brilliant, just reasonably intelligent. Every business student you have has the requisite intelligence and requisite energy. Integrity is not hard wired into your DNA. A student at that age can pretty much decide what kind a person they are going to be at sixty. If they don't have integrity, they*

never will. The chains of habit are sometimes too heavy to be broken. Students can forge their own chains. Just pick a person to admire and ask why you admire them, usually it is because they are generous, decent, kind people, and those are the kind of people to emulate."

When I was young, things were different.

The first car I ever bought in 1964 was the best deal I ever made, because I took my Uncle Walter along. It was a used car owned by "Dapper Dan," who had a dealership in Richmond Virginia at the time. He had a big street sign with his picture in it wearing a top hat, and it said: "I'd Give the Cars Away but My Wife Won't Let Me." Walter recommended that I go there to look, because he said he could always con a con; he could tell by the sign. So, we visited the dealership during closing hours and looked through the inventory. I spotted a 1956 Plymouth that I liked with a $1,200 price tab.

Two days before we went to buy, Walter sent his cleaning lady there to make a low-ball offer on the car, to get into Damper Dan's head a bit. She let Dan tell his story and then offered him $700, which he politely refused, but then she walked out without making a counter leaving Dan wondering. The next morning Walter sent in a mechanic-friend of his who talked the car down and pointed out all the things wrong with it, before making an offer of only $400. According to his expert testimony, the engine was so worn out that all the pistons would have to be replaced within a month and cost $800; Dan didn't blink, and the mechanic left carless. Nonetheless, the "mark" was confused by the two front runners, and he was probably ready to dump the Plymouth before we even got there. But, to make sure, the night before we went to do a deal, Walter and I drove over to the deserted lot, and he poured some oil on the asphalt under the engine block.

"What's that for?" I asked.

"To out-dapper the Dan", he replied.

First thing the next morning, we were dropped off by a friend and wandered listlessly among the array of automobiles until we stopped at the blue Plymouth. After looking at it all around and up and down, Dapper Dan came out of the dealership door, smiling, with his top hat on and two cokes in his hand, ready to nail two suckers.

"What-cha looking for guys? I've got more cars than I know what to do with and need to make a sale today to pay my electric bill before the electricity is cut off."

Walter pointed to me and replied: "The kid here wants a car to drive, to deliver papers on his paper route in the morning, but he doesn't have much money. What do you suggest?"

"Well, I can make you a great deal on that blue Plymouth you are standing next to: It was owned by an 80-year- old lady who kept it in the garage most of the time, and only drove it to church on Sunday and the orphanage on Saturday, where she did volunteer work. Her eyesight went bad and she can't drive at night, so I bought it from her after communion last month; we go to the same church you know."

"She sounds like a good Christian woman, is she single?" Walter quipped, with his Methuselahian-smile. Without waiting for an answer, he turned his back on me and lowered his voice to Dapper Dan, so I could barely hear.

"His mother died several years ago, and his dad has cancer and can't work. If he doesn't keep up his paper route, he can't stay in school. All he's got is six hundred and thirty-seven dollars, and I'm on social security and can't help or I would. I guess he will have to save some more money and come back in a couple months, 'cuz he certainly needs a dependable car like that Plymouth...besides, I think it is leaking oil."

Startled, the Dan looked under the front end and saw the puddle. Red-faced and with visions of being piston-poor, he blurted: "I swear I had my mechanic check it out from top to bottom and the engine was clean; you have my double-D guarantee on that."

Looking skeptical, Walter replied: "Well, I'd be willing to take a chance on it if you will take $637 and throw in five free oil changes for the kid...maybe you could call your wife and see if she will let you do the deal." Dapper nodded so quickly his hat went cock-eyed and he scurried to the office.

Now...we both knew that he didn't call his wife, and why Dapper Dan took our offer, but he didn't know that he had been had by the master, my Uncle Walter. As we drove away in the car, Walter said: "Let that be a lesson to you son: always leave a sucker thinking that you were the sucker, you might need him again one day. Like when the Plymouth stops running." I never forgot that advice and it has saved me thousands of dollars in deals over my lifetime, and I made some dapper friends along the way. They never knew what they didn't know... And, now you know.

Millennials today are no suckers; therefore, businesses need to know how to sell them because millennials have overtaken boomers as America's largest generation (74M strong). Here is some advice in that regard:

1. Don't give them a sales pitch. The slick salesman is out of style. Younger customers don't want a sales talk, they want unbiased information about products and services. That's why they trust comments by other millennials on social media more than company representatives or commercials on TV.

2. Your brand is important to them, but don't make it all about you. Millennials like conducting business with brands that get a lot of "likes;" brands that focus less on a mission statement and more on what they do. Avoid blowing your own horn because millennials are turned-off by that. This population segment doesn't care about how long you've been in business, how big your company is, or what you think is important. They care about how you treat them, how well you keep your promises and the value your brand adds to their lives.

3. Be personal. Like everyone else, millennials like doing business with other people. If you don't remember this, you could lose their business. Use technology to makes it possible to get to the right people in the company quickly, who can solve their problem. Millennials don't like to do business with faceless corporations; they prefer transparency and attention, not phone messages that say "We appreciate your call, stay on the line and a representative will be with you" ... followed by a 15 minute wait. If you appreciated them, you wouldn't make them wait 15 minutes to talk to someone. Millennials are impatient.

4. Make it a good experience. If millennials have a bad experience with your business, they are likely to post a bad review on Yelp or Facebook and your business can't afford the negative publicity. Therefore, make the customer service experience a priority. Handle customer complaints and problems like your business depended on it.

5. Get connected. To reach the most connected group of consumers in the world, your business needs to be connected to them with a mobile app and social media. That means you need to be mobile — offering an enticing experience through smartphones and social media. Don't be afraid to "chat" and interact with them. But remember: If every interaction with you is a sales pitch, you'll turn them off and they'll look elsewhere.

6. Presentation is important. Millennials consume media all day, every day and they're used to seeing highly polished images, well-produced video and other visual media. However, don't forget the value of real content—blowing your own horn is not content, it's arrogance.

7. You want them to tell their friends about you. Although millennials will likely write a bad review of your business if they have a bad experience, they're likely to rave about you if you provide outstanding customer service or your product works better than advertised. They were raised sharing great experiences with their friends.

Once upon a time I was the same age as millennials and I had a father that led and inspired; we often talked about serious matters that he prefaced with this advice: "I've already gone where you are going, so look at me and see yourself tomorrow." He empowered me at a young age by sharing his problems and asking: "What do you think?"

I've been thinking about problems ever since and looking for solutions, and I do believe that any serious discussion must start with "What do you think?" Then you must listen to the response.

Millennials today may be socially connected like never before, but they're not intellectually challenged by serious, face-to-face conversation. Following the "likes" is fostering a herd mentality which negates independent thinking; nevertheless, millennials are a herd that a business can't afford to ignore. Invest in the grass and water right in front of the herd's direction and you will make a lot of money.

Millennials like Bitcoin. For example, singer Katy Perry recently asked Warren Buffett about cryptocurrency and he answered, "Stay away from it. It's a mirage, basically. The idea that it has some huge intrinsic value is a joke in my view. I don't believe in this whole thing at all. I think it's going to implode."

However, Warren never met a millennial he agreed with. Katy has 68M followers on Instagram and she has influence, perhaps enough to drive Bitcoin up another few thousand dollars. Maybe she will write a song about it. Nonetheless, Buffet has a $68B net worth and some influence also—at least with me. I agree with him: "It's a joke…. and it's going to implode."

The idea that Bitcoin could ever be a currency is flawed, simply because it defies the crucial element of a currency: that coin be a consistent store of value and medium of exchange. How would you price something for sale in Bitcoins, when the price fluctuates 50% a month? It would require ten-minute price re-tagging at Macy's.

Cryptocurrency is really a cliptocurrency and you are likely going to get clipped if you hold it too long. What is too long? That is a question only implosion can answer. In the meantime, trading was so heavy in January that many Bitcoin exchanges shut down for a time: the GDAX, Gemini and Kraken all had trouble causing the price to fall a $1,000 from 3:30 to 5PM one day in December. All in a day's work for a Bitcoin trader.

Like I said, I was once the same age as millennials today and drifted longer than most. In the summer of 1972, I was working as a tennis instructor during the day and a waiter at night in South Lake Tahoe. It was a hedonistic way of life mainly focused on girls and sports, and it was sure fun. I was twenty-four years old at the time and searching for a path to a more secure future. I didn't really know which way to go, having dropped out of college my junior year in search of adventure. I found it on the ski slopes, and in the casinos and beautiful outdoors of Tahoe, but hedonism grows on you like an addiction, until it is ruined by financial reality. And that summer a collision occurred in my life.

I was teaching tennis at a development called Lake Village which housed a few hundred luxury condos, and one of the owners, a 50-year-old woman, approached me for lessons. Her name was Lorraine. She had never picked up a racquet before, but her husband had always played and goaded her into learning to play.

After a few sessions that made me suspect she had no athletic ability whatsoever, she asked: "What do you think? Will I ever learn to hit the ball over the net?"

I replied: "Lorraine, I really think you should take a week off to reflect and then give it up all together. This is not baseball, you don't get three swings to hit the ball."

She beamed a smile and said: "Thank you so much, will you tell my husband that? I hate tennis. Come to dinner tonight so you can break the news to him. He will want to know the specifics because he is a detail person."

"O...kay," I said. What else could I say after putting her down so hard?

As fate would have it, her husband turned out to be a nice guy. He was about five-foot three, 74 years old and looked like Yoda, but he never raised his voice when I told him about his wife's tennis. In fact, after dinner, he asked me to help him with a math crossword puzzle because he didn't see so well, and I did. Even though my grades in school rarely showed it, I was always good with numbers and I gave him a few right answers that night—at least enough that he invited me back to dinner two days later.

In between dinners, I happened to read in the paper an article about a billionaire named A. N. Pritzker, who owned all the Hyatt Hotels, 150 other companies—and who was one of the biggest landowners in the United States. I knew Lorraine's last name was Pritzker, and I heard her call her husband A.N., so in my next visit I told the old man about the billionaire with the same name as him.

He said, "Yeah, that's me, I can't get away from reporters who report my every move; I hate it."

"What are you doing in this condo, if you are so rich?" I asked

He replied, "My wife loves Tahoe. The summer is great, so we come here every July. Besides, I own Lake Village."

At first, I was flabbergasted—me doing puzzles with a billionaire?

Then I became curious and asked: "How did you make all that money?"

"Well, I graduated from Harvard law school in 1922, but never practiced. My brother Jack became a CPA but stopped practicing when we went into the real estate business together in the 1920s. The business just grew; and boy, did we pick up some deals in the depression. To be successful, you've got to know accounting and law."

Two months later I went back to college and changed majors from history to accounting, taking 18 credits a semester and graduating in a year: I did nothing but study and left hedonism behind, cold turkey. I came out of the fog that year and I knew that I wanted to learn to invest like A.N. Pritzker. That's how I got started in business. Forty years later, I'm still trying to learn to invest like A.N. Pritzker.

Retirement

About one-third of Americans retire and claim their Social Security benefits as soon as they become eligible at age 62, and end up dying faster than if they just kept working (M. Fitzpatrick, Cornell University). Retirement is ranked 10th on the list of life's 43 most stressful events because work is a big part of a person's social life. Additionally, if you are not financially secure, then leaving the security of a paycheck can be depressing and life-shortening. A Harvard study also found that retirees were 40% more likely to have a heart attack than those that kept working after age 65.

In other words, all the research points to working longer and delaying Social Security benefits. If you've got to retire, join a Zumba class, or go back to school and take classes. You will live longer, but not as long as if you continue to work into your seventies. A job is the best thing that ever happened to you; it may take retirement to realize that. A retired person can take just so many ocean cruises before all the buffets look the same.

As example of a successful retiree, my great Uncle Walter died about 50 years ago at age 87 or so. He rented a room in a boarding house in Richmond, Virginia, until he keeled over with a heart attack one day while fishing on the Chickahominy River—what he did every day the last half of his life. He fished from dawn to dusk and he loved it. In his earlier life, Walter was a very successful businessman until he retired at age 47. Still, he drove a ten-year-old Chevy, ate breakfast at the same two-bit restaurant every morning and never ordered any drink except water just to save a dime. He never left a tip either, but the waitresses treated him like royalty, because he always told them a joke when they brought him a meal and made them laugh. Walter appeared to have everything except money; at least that is the way I saw it, when he took me fishing on my tenth birthday.

When he picked me up at my grandmother's house in central Richmond, early in the morning, I thought it odd that he walked the block to his car along the edge of the street gutter while looking down the whole time. Curiously, I looked with him and had to ask what we were looking for, and he said: "Change, I found a quarter over on Broad Street yesterday.

People don't know how to hold on to money; it falls out of their pockets when they get out of the car and into the gutter."

His simple strategy of frugality struck home that day—after that, I often looked down while walking, because I learned from Walter that keeping my head down could put a jingle in my pocket. That message was ratified when Walter died; in settling his estate we found that he was a rich man. Walter knew how to mother a dollar and be happy at the same time and that ability has been lost in our society today, which follows the Kardashian creed: "Money is not worth having unless the whole world knows you have it." I prefer Walter's habit when it comes to money, marked by a jingle. Having money doesn't make you rich, holding on to it does.

It is a no-jingle world and most people must rely on the government one day. Around 90% of all individuals aged 65 and older report that Social Security benefits are their important source of income, representing more than 34% of total income for baby boomers that retire (MarketWatch 5-3-2017). In addition, company sponsored 401k plans and personal savings are two additional elements necessary for retirement. In other words, Social Security will never be enough and you should save by increasing your salary deferrals into a retirement plan or IRA. In addition, there is a growing trend for people to continue working until age 70 or longer, to minimize hitting their retirement accounts too early. The segment of those over the age of 65 in the labor force is now 18.8%, up from 12.8% in 2000 (AARP). Few people are currently on a savings path that will let them retire in their 60s. They will work longer and probably live on less than their parents did in retirement. In 1970, 37% of the workforce had a company pension to count on; today only 7% do.

There is also a trend to be more invested in equities after age 65, because people are living longer and wish to continue building their portfolios, going after a high return. I disagree with that endeavor, however, because of the risk; stocks can go down and stay down longer than a baby boomer can stay alive. At some point, everyone must quit working and live off their portfolio, but at least you can count on what you've saved if the investments are safe. My advice is to take the market risk if you have a decade or so longer to work; after that, don't risk it. Dreams of a big return in the stock market can become a nightmare, if you are not young enough to work through it.

When you retire, you must learn about Medicare and it isn't cheap. However, if the supply of doctors was increased by cutting tuition in half with subsidies, and there were more medical schools, fees would go down. That can't be done because the AMA won't license more schools, monopolizing the supply of doctors to keep their pay from falling. Nonetheless, the docs should be made to publish a price list and compete for customers like every other business does—then Medicaid, Medicare or Blue Cross should pay whatever the bill is, after the insured pays a co-pay and puts some skin in the game. The price for service will be the lowest it can get with a free market, because consumers would shop around for the lowest price if they could Google it. Currently they can't.

Why shouldn't the federal government mandate coverages so that people know what they are getting without having to fathom the fine print? With home-owner policies for example, there are three standard policies now—HO1, HO2 and HO3—and coverages are mandated and priced accordingly in a competitive insurance market. That's private insurance in a government-regulated environment and it works. The government sets the rules and the market competes for the business. Without regulations, the public gets screwed by corporate greed. Without the free market, the public gets screwed by government intervention and inefficiency. The problem with the medical system is that the government is operating an insurance business and it shouldn't; the medical industry doesn't do business in a free market and it should. Free up supply and unharness demand with price- competition, and a "regulated" market will make healthcare cost efficient and effective.

There is also no common sense in medicine, for example:

There was an old geezer, who had been a retired doctor for a long time; a he became very bored and decided to open a medical clinic. He put a sign up that said: "Dr. Geezer's clinic. Get your treatment for $500, if not cured get back $1,000." There was a young doctor down the street who knew all the latest technology and had a staff that could bill insurance companies and Medicare with computerized impunity; a cash-on-the-barrel-head doctor was a threat to his professional existence, not to mention the AMA was alarmed at the geezer's money back guarantee. I will call the young doc "Dr. Young." He was positive that the old geezer didn't know beans about modern medicine and thought that he would show him up and make a $1,000 to boot. So, he went to Dr. Geezer's clinic and posed as a patient with no insurance:

Dr. Young: Dr. Geezer, I have lost all taste in my mouth. Can you please help me?

Dr. Geezer: Nurse, please bring medicine from box 22 and put 3 drops in Dr. Young's mouth.

Dr. Young: Aaagh! This is gasoline!

Dr. Geezer: Congratulations! You've got your taste back. That will be $500.

Dr. Young gets annoyed and goes back after a couple of days figuring to recover his money.

Dr. Young: I have lost my memory, I cannot remember anything.

Dr. Geezer: Nurse, please bring medicine from box 22 and put 3 drops in the patient's mouth.

Doctor Young: Oh no you don't—that is gasoline!

Dr. Geezer: Congratulations! You've got your memory back. That will be $500.

Dr. Young (after having lost $1000) leaves angrily and comes back after several more days.

Dr. Young: My eyesight has become weak—I can hardly see!

Dr. Geezer: Well, I don't have any medicine for that so Here's your $1000 back.

Dr. Young: But this is only $500...

Dr. Geezer: Congratulations! You got your vision back! That will be $500.

Immigration & Employment

Email From: R
Sent: Monday, October 23, 2017 2:57 PM
To: Alan Moore
Subject: Re: Robots taking over

R: "I don't understand the points you are making. If computers are eliminating jobs at the breakneck speed you keep saying, why do we need more immigrants when the robots are going to be doing the work? A local dairy farm just laid off his entire Mexican crew and kept 3 people to milk his entire herd. Now we have 40 unemployed Mexicans all applying for unemployment. New York State being the land of socialism, they will now either collect unemployment or welfare OR BOTH. Everything you write bashes automation eliminating jobs at astronomical rates which makes sense that you would want to save what jobs that are left to Americans. "

On Mon, Oct 23, 2017 at 9:49 AM, Alan Moore <alanm@slavic401k.com> responded:

"In Reagan's era there were 144m people of working age; when George Bush was President there were 162M, which is about what we have now. But, Trump is decreasing legal immigration by 75% by executive order, which is expected to cause an 18M fall in the number of workers over the next 10 years, along with all the baby boomers checking out of employment and retiring at the rate of 10k per day. At the same time, the birth rate is falling. The bottom line is: you can't create employment if there are fewer people of working age to be employed. It is demographically impossible. And, if, somehow, we are able to attract 72-yr-olds back into the workforce, productivity will go down. Before Social Security came into existence in 1935, 50% of men never retired, but today only 13% of people over the age of 65 keep working. There aren't enough young workers to keep supporting all the old people on Social Security, especially if you cut immigration by 75%. We need those immigrants climbing up the ladder of success and paying payroll taxes. The tax bill won't fix those issues, nor does it deal with the future: more robots will take away more jobs in the continuing drive for efficiency. After Trump is long gone, the rich will still have to pay more and the bottom half will have to take less—less and less with the tax-bill that passed, calling for a $1.5T tax cut—for who knows whom—and the 1.5T deficit it creates because the cuts are not paid for by eliminating deductions. That 1.5T deficit is on top of the 5T already projected as a 10-yr deficit."

As the economy advances into 2018, demographics and the technology revolution are the tip of the next recession unless we have a skilled workforce ready to go. We don't. What we do have is more money not going into capital investment, but into the stock market and passing through public companies into the pockets of the shareholders with stock buybacks and dividends. That begs the question: does more money flowing to the top 1% create jobs, or do higher wages create more jobs that create money flowing to everyone else? The answer: It really doesn't matter if capital investment and jobs continue to be outsourced to China or allocated to automation. Without jobs, a tax cut can only benefit the people who are paying the taxes in the first place. In that regard, the top 1% pay 40% of the taxes. Therefore, the odds are 40 to 1 on who will benefit the most from the cuts.

A much bigger impact than taxes is coming from automation. In the *Financial Times* on 10-23-17, page 7, is a story about what Nike is doing with its 450,000 employees in 15 low-wage countries—where it outsourced production decades ago...it's eliminating 30% of those jobs with robots using the new "Flex" process which will add 5% to earnings per share. Jae-Hee Chang said: "After 'Flex' there will still be jobs for people who can troubleshoot and work alongside robots."

There will always be a demand for skilled labor—at least until the robots learn more skills.

Still, everybody knows that automation is going to take half the jobs over the next 30 or 40 years, but what they don't realize is the socio-economic consequence. At first, the machines will target expensive labor to increase profits—and there will be no replacement jobs except low-paying ones that are not worth automating, like picking fruit. With wages being eliminated, aggregate demand will decrease dramatically, forcing prices to fall and profits as well, leading business "back to the future." The question will become: "Sell what to whom?" No one has an answer to that question.

The first companies to automate will kill the competition, like Amazon has done to retailers. Amazon.com has been bragging about plans to create 100k jobs in 2018, but for every job Amazon creates, it destroys two or three others. Amazon has revolutionized the way Americans consume, but to retail workers, Amazon is a graveyard. Between Macy's, Sears, Kmart and JC Penny's, 125,000 retail workers been laid off over the past two years alone.

The end game of automation is to kill jobs, which depreciates humanity as an unintended consequence. When automation is complete, there is only one democratic outcome that works politically and economically in addressing the huge unemployment problem that will occur: Transfer ownership of the machines to the unemployed majority so that they can live off the dividend income.

Therefore, if we don't find the answer to this problem, it will mean the end of capitalism as we know it. That's why the middle class is so important, with their larger-than-average wages. The middle class will vote to leave the economic system intact, as long as they have something to lose. Accordingly, a tax-cut that primarily lands in the top five-percenter's pockets and causes greater income inequality, will undermine capitalism, not help it—because the middle class will get smaller as the race to automate heats up.

Socially, the solution is for wider ownership of public companies that pay dividends, like what is happening with participants in 401k plans. However, the culture is to spend, not save, and that is what the Fed has caused by keeping rates too low for so long. Stock buybacks, mergers, acquisitions and bubbles don't inspire confidence either. They kill jobs.

Baby Boomers

The fact is, the average 401k account balance of a 65-year-old is less than 50k, which should give you an idea when the average baby boomer can afford to retire: right after he is dead. That's the new retirement age. If the retiree lives past his life expectancy, his average real expenditures will increase due to medical costs, though they do not necessarily exceed their initial retirement levels until retirees reach their mid-nineties. The irony is, in the first year the retiree usually goes on a spending spree that David Blanchett labels the "Spending Smile." A person would have to save $1,020,000 by age 65 to live this way at a 4% payout rate, after considering the $2,400 per month that social security would provide in addition.

For a 35-year-old aiming to live until 94, that requires a savings rate of $1,075 per month for 30 years to get to retirement, if a 6% return is continually earned until 65—at which time market risk must be reduced and a 3 or 4% return is more likely. Saving a thousand dollars a month is often hard to do at age 35, especially if you are only making 50k at the time and have a family. At age 55, you will probably make twice as much, but if you wait until then to start saving, there is no hope. For the typical baby boomer today, there is no hope for a "spending smile" in the hereafter. How much money is enough? When John D. Rockefeller was asked that question he answered: "Just a little more." Any way you cut it, saving big is tough and you should always save a "little more."

In her book *Nomadland*, Jessica Bruder reveals the dark, depressing and physically painful life of a tribe of men and women in their 60s, who have taken to living in RVs and vans and driving from one place to another to pick up seasonal low-wage jobs. Driven from their homes by a lack of savings or a steady job, these people are often living on less than a 1,000 a month, working temp-gigs at places like Amazon and picking fruit for farmers. For them, when it comes to retirement, 65 is the new 50, because they must do hard labor in order to survive; and there are tens of thousands of them wondering about. Amazon often employs old folks to work alongside the robots in distribution centers because no one else will do the monotonous tasks, giving them 15-minute breaks that take 15 minutes to walk to the bathroom and back—so far, so tiring; it gets old fast. This is the new American "Gulag."

The graph that follows provides a projection by David Blanchett of Morningstar on typical spending when a retiree begins retirement with expenditures of $100,000/yr, which was his/her ending salary. On average, this household can expect to experience declining real expenditures through age eighty-four, when real spending reaches a trough of $74,146, which is a 26% drop in spending gradually over 17 years.

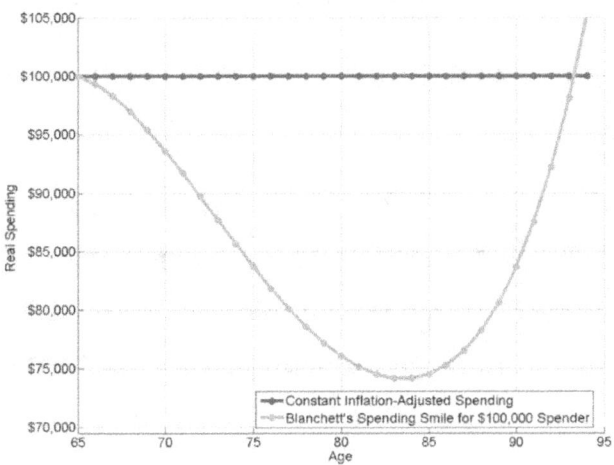

One thing is for sure: age catches up with you fast if you don't have money, and charity starts at home, your home. Save a little more because frugality works.

It also runs in my family—saving money is a lifelong commitment like my great-uncle Edgar and his wife Regina made. They lived on a farm twenty miles east of Richmond, Virginia, during the first half of the twentieth century, and they saved every dime, more to the credit of Regina than Edgar, who always liked to live-it-up a little—but she wore the pants in the family. When Uncle Edgar hit 70 years old in the early 1940s, he really wanted to fly in an airplane just once before he died; and he would say to his wife every year at the county fair where plane rides were offered for $20: "Regina, let's take a ride before we go to seed."

And she would reply, "No way, twenty dollars is twenty dollars."

At the fair in 1947, after hearing his wife give him the "twenty dollars is twenty dollars" excuse for six years, Edgar was offered a deal by the pilot of the old, open-cockpit, bi-plane used to take customers for a spin.

He said: "I'll take you and your wife up for free if neither one of you say a word the whole trip; otherwise, you have to pay me the twenty dollars."

Even Regina couldn't say no to a free ride, so they buckled-up and took off. The pilot commenced to do all sorts of flying tricks, loop-to-loops and such, trying to get a sound out of the couple, but he didn't hear a word until he landed. Looking back, he only saw Edgar and no Regina.

"What happened to Regina?" he yelled.

"She fell out the first loop you did," Edgar said calmly.

"Why didn't you say something?" the pilot said incredulously.

"Well, she was gone—nothing I could do about that, and twenty dollars is twenty dollars." Edgar lived comfortably the rest of his life, in more ways than one.

Conscientious people like Edgar and Regina don't buy things on impulse, or spend too much money, or buy things they don't really need—they save diligently for retirement. To boot, it is the personality trait most closely related to academic achievement, job performance, marital stability and longevity. "Conscientious people accumulate more wealth than less conscientious people, even after accounting for differences in income, education and cognitive ability." (MarketWatch, 5-10-17)

Psychologically, there is certain comfort in maintaining a wall between capital and income—never spend your capital—conscientious objectors say, however, in retirement that wall must come down, because most people can only afford to take an annual 4% payout from their retirement account to supplement Social Security and not run out of money in their lifetime—if their genes are normal. This payout plan should be composed of a combination of dividends/interest and capital—if risk control is an objective—which mandates underweighting market exposure in retirement. In other words, it's good to be conscientious all the way through life and there are a couple of indicators: do you pay off your credit card(s) off completely every month? Are you never late for an appointment? Do you change the oil in your car when the little sticker on the windshield says so? Little things go a long way toward preserving capital.

My Uncle Walter was conscientious and couldn't stand owing anybody a dime: he often paid his electric bill a month in advance and then turned off all the lights until the bill came showing a credit balance. Then he would call American Electric Power and demand payment of his loan and hit them up for some interest. They always paid it to get rid of him, because he threatened to go public and call the *Richmond Times-Dispatch* with the story. He would spin the headline for AEP's billing department: "Power Company Defaults on Loan." Uncle Walter always got his nickel's worth and saved the first nickel he ever made at the age of ten, back in 1895. He carried it everywhere he went and died with that nickel in his pocket, because he was always proud of his "nickel and dime" reputation. He once showed me that nickel, when I was a boy, and told me how he made it. We both laughed and I never forgot the story.

In the group of kids he hung around with, he was thought to be a weirdo, rarely talking, always listening intently. The other boys liked to tease him, thinking he was stupid. So, they played a trick on him over and over just for laughs: they would offer him a choice between a nickel and a dime, and he always picked the nickel, saying it was a better deal because the coin was bigger—and the kids got a kick out of it. I asked Walter why he kept picking the nickel, and he said: "If I picked the dime they would have stopped doing it, and I made $20 off them in nickels before they all finally went broke. I kept that first nickel to remind me to never underestimate the stupidity of the public, and I made a lot of money that way over my career."

Learning much from Walter, when people ask me how to make a million bucks in the stock market with little risk, I tell them to start with two million, because they are probably going to lose half of it by trading. I know a little about business, but very little about the future of stock prices; investing is a risk that I choose not to take unless the odds are heavily in my favor. A market that is 25 times earnings is not in my favor and I am often amazed how smart business people often think they will automatically be smart in something else, like investing in stocks, bonds and real estate when they made their pile in manufacturing. With the markets making a new high every other day in December of 2017, investors are thinking "so far, so good." However, that idiom was plagiarized from an old rumor originating when Charles Dow accidently fell off a twenty-story building on Wall Street in 1902; and as he fell, the people on each floor could hear him say:

so far, so good; so far, so good. Most investment theories die hard, but Dow's investment theory is a thing of the past.

Apart from his theory, Dow did make some profound observations about investing, such as: "For an investor, who must take risks in order to make money; who will buy nothing without careful, thorough investigation; and who will not risk more than he is able to lose, there is no other investment in the world today as tempting as stocks."

Some things never change and today, stocks are just as tempting as ever. There are many theories of investing, but none more popular that Modern Portfolio Theory (MPT), which was introduced by Nobel Prize winner Harry Markowitz in a 1952 article. The fundamental concept behind MPT is that the assets in a portfolio should not be selected individually; there should only be two investments in a portfolio: a stock index fund coupled with risk-free Treasury bills depending on one's risk tolerance. According to Markowitz, efficient investing entails a tradeoff between risk and expected return, and stock picking and market-timing are a waste of time, because they introduce non-systematic risk without yielding a higher return than the market itself. Most studies since 1952 indicate that 80% of investment managers do not keep up with the S&P index every year; therefore, it makes little sense to buy a managed mutual fund or hire an investment manager to pick stocks: the added expense is not worth the expected return.

Following that logic, MPT is a form of diversification that generates the highest expected, risk-related return possible. Without a complex statistical model to compute the appropriate allocation, a quick rule of thumb is the "rule of 100": subtract the investor's age from 100 and invest the answer in an index fund and the rest in a short-term, government bond fund. This strategy also requires that the portfolio be rebalanced every year on one's birthday, or if the risk profile should change.

Always a stumbling block, there is a credibility gap between having a successful career and being a good investor; it is called ego and you must be able to suppress it.

My Uncle Walter pointed out the ego gap to me early on with this story about Calvin Coolidge. President Coolidge stopped at a gas station in 1926 near Richmond and Walter happened to be there drinking a coke at the time. It was a hot summer day. According to the papers, Coolidge had met with Harvey Firestone, Thomas Edison and Henry Ford and they went for a drive to get out of Washington and test out the new Ford model. The station attendant became interested in the new car as he pumped the gas, and they all got out, except Coolidge, who was driving.

Firestone said to the attendant: "Do you see those tires? I made them."

Then Edison said: "Do you see that electrical equipment? I invented it."

Then Ford said: "See that car? I made it."

The attendant grinned, not quite believing it all, and said, "Get outta here—the next thing you'll be telling me is that guy behind the wheel is the President of the United States!"

As Walter always said: "Success grows an ego, but it's best to mind your own business keep your mouth shut."

Calvin sure did and was known as a man of few words. One time, a reporter caught him in a hallway and tried to get him to comment on some new legislation by saying: "Mr. President, I bet my editor that I could get you to say more than two words."

Coolidge replied: "You lose" and walked on.

Cal reduced the national debt 26%, ran a budget surplus four years in a row and cut income taxes 20%, while growing GDP 10% a year. The economy roared back then, and Cal kept his mouth shut about it the whole time.

As far as making a million bucks is concerned, Firestone, Edison and Ford never bought a stock other than in their own businesses and they did okay with them. Here they are together in a picture in 1929.

To wit, in 1910, Henry Ford astonished the world by doubling wages to $5 per day in his Michigan plants in one day. He even dropped the work day to eight hours from nine and the business community thought he would go bankrupt, but the move proved extremely profitable; instead of constant turnover of employees, the best mechanics in the country flocked to Detroit, bringing in their human capital and expertise and raising productivity. Using the CPI index, Henry's $5-wage equals about $150 a day in 2015 dollars. The industrial revolution brought a wage revolution, much like the tech revolution happening today...particularly at Amazon.

The Economy

Marketwatch 1-18-18: "The U.S. is seeing the tightest labor market in decades; workers are finding something that's long been missing from the broader economic expansion: faster-growing paychecks. Workers in metro areas with the lowest unemployment are experiencing the strongest wage growth in the country. The labor market in places like Minneapolis, Denver and Fort Myers, Fla., where unemployment rates stand near or even below 3%, has now tightened to a point where businesses are raising pay to attract employees, often from competitors. It's an outcome entirely expected in economic theory, but one that's been largely absent until now in the upturn that began more than eight years ago."

There are two forces fighting it out for the direction of the economy and interest rates: Technology is driving deflation and tight labor is instigating inflation. Long-term GDP depends on growth in the workforce and productivity growth. However, technology is not only a substitution for labor, but also for bricks and mortar. Any company that doesn't have a capital-light strategy going forward will be left behind the competition, because software and automation are driving profit margins. Therefore, tax cuts, full employment and deficit spending will have a muted effect on growth. The expansion of technology is at the expense of everything else, when it comes to job creation and wages. Is anyone building a new mall these days? Walmart is closing 63 stores and Macy's a ton more. The S&P is trading at 26 times earnings (Barron's, 1-13-18, p. M35), which is evidence in the faith in technology, because the tech sector is 22% of the S&P and higher than it has been since year 2000, right before the NASDAQ crashed.

Education

President Trump announced a new bill that would restrict the issuance of green cards and H-1B visas by 50%. Currently about a million people a year get green cards. His reason for doing this is to help the low-income American workers who get jobs taken away by immigrants that will work for less. That may well be the case, but the best case is to educate and train Americans to do the jobs of the future—in STEM. In that regard, our schools are going downhill because of lax parenting and because the teachers' unions protect bad teaching, which holds down the pay of the good teachers because of the "no teacher left behind" policy when it comes to negotiating pay raises with the local school boards. It's communism in the classroom, as all the teachers get the same raise and no child is allowed to flunk without a committee's review.

An excellent teacher should be paid like an NFL running back, if America's culture was in the right place. What follows is an "excellent" teacher's point of view on the subject, explaining the attitude of students today and the culture they live in. The problem is not too many green cards; it's grey matter, like in brains.

Dr. Richard Hattendorf, a retired professor, emailed me this in 2013: "...A grade is just a symbol of recognition of the value of the performance. In brief, I have come to suspect that many college students are teenagers or, worse, children, who are not at all prepared by grade and high school for university, or, finally for life as adults. They blame the professor and complain to the Dean because Mom and Dad will back them up most of the time; after all, their parents pay the bills. In my day (I really sound like an old man here), my father would look at me sternly and ask me what I did to get such a bad grade, and go over the work, or lack of it. He did not blame the teacher... he was more interested in my understanding the material and performing well. He knew the grades would come if I did just that; and it was my responsibility to study until I understood the material—or get help...not just slide through and put the blame on others. Also, I was taught that if I did not do the work or did it poorly, the consequences would not be pretty...and I would have to deal with that, with failure. Failure taught one something: work harder and try to avoid it, if possible.

Lacking this work ethic and lacking a sense of personal responsibility for failure and success, is producing a tragedy in America."

That's the other side of the education story and the message is clear: you learn just as much from failure as you do from success and protecting your child from failure is a "neglect of duty." What's missing from the classroom is a microcosm of what's lacking in the nation. It is culture's fault. Culture begins in the home and stays with you forever. Good culture is failsafe.

I saw a new movie called *Gifted* in 2017 and it got me thinking. So, I did a little research. In Malcom Gladwell's book, *Outliers*, he studied the relationship between success and IQ and found that a high IQ does not generally correlate to higher achievement, because once a person's IQ is above 120, a relationship between the two doesn't exist. Someone with an IQ of 125 isn't any less likely to win a Nobel Prize than someone with an IQ of 170. He also concluded that to become truly skilled in any activity, you must work at it for 10,000 hours, which is roughly five years.

Millennials should take note and stick to some gainful employment no matter how boring it is; and give yourself a chance to develop a career. It doesn't take smarts, it takes persistence.

Gladwell focused on the guy who had the highest IQ ever recorded, Chris Langam with an IQ of 195 –that's thirty percent higher than Albert Einstein's. Langam learned to speak when he was only six months old, and his prodigious intelligence continued to make itself known throughout his childhood and adolescence. He earned a perfect score on the SAT despite taking a nap during the test; he attended Montana State University only to drop out believing that he could teach his professors more than they could teach him. After dropping out, Langam took a string of labor-intensive jobs for some time, and by his mid-40s had been a construction worker, farmhand, and, for over twenty years, a bouncer on Long Island.

In another study by Lewis Terman, a psychology professor at Stanford University, it was determined that child geniuses do not turn out the way people imagine. Many were successful, but many were not. Most led normal middle-class lives, and none of them became famous for anything. And, in fact, two children he had rejected for the study, because their IQs were too low, went on to win Nobel prizes. The lesson learned from Terman is that to say a person is a genius is not saying much.

Gladwell and Terman confirm what Calvin Coolidge said about success: "Nothing in the world can take the place of persistence...Genius will not; most geniuses never reach a fraction of their potential." So went Langam, the smartest guy on the planet.

Education is the most important element in developing skilled workers and the American education system is not working. Following are the student rankings worldwide. The important thing is where America is on the charts versus China, Korea, Japan and Germany. Those countries maintain a trade surplus with the United States—do you see the correlation? Those countries are holding a big portion of our national debt resulting from their favorable trade balance, meaning they are getting richer at our expense. Whose GDP is increasing the fastest? China's. Where did Japan go wrong with so many smart kids?

Their government borrowed too much after the bubbles popped in the early 1990s—Japan invented the 100-year mortgage which sent real estate prices to $2,000 a square foot. Easy money will do the same thing to China one day, but at least they are developing the brains to pick up the pieces, and they have $2.4 trillion in reserves. The US can't pick up the slack in growth because we are at the bottom of the chart and the country has too much debt.

To add an anecdote to the graph: Where I live in Palm Beach County, 99.9% of the 13,000 teachers get the highest marks available every year; usually, only four or five score below standard, but all 13,000 get the same 2 or 3% raise. However, Florida's schools consistently rank in the bottom quartile in the nation, which means the average Florida student falls off the chart below, ranking just above Rwanda in Africa.

Mathematics

	Mean score		55.4%
Shanghai-China	613		
Singapore	573		
Chinese Taipei	560		
Hong Kong-China	561		
Korea	554		
Liechtenstein	535		
Macao-China	538		
Japan	536		
Switzerland	531		
Belgium	515		
Netherlands	523		
Germany	514		
Poland	518		
Canada	518		
Finland	519		
New Zealand	500		
Australia	504		
Estonia	521		
Austria	506		
Slovenia	501		
Viet Nam	511		
France	495		
Czech Republic	499		
OECD average	494		
United Kingdom	494		
Luxembourg	490		
Iceland	493		
Slovak Republic	482		
Ireland	501		
Portugal	487		
Denmark	500		
Italy	485		
Norway	489		
Israel	466		
Hungary	477		
United States	481		

Science

	Mean score	
Shanghai-China	580	
Singapore	551	
Japan	547	
Finland	545	
Hong Kong-China	555	
Australia	521	
New Zealand	516	
Estonia	541	
Germany	524	
Netherlands	522	
Korea	538	
Canada	525	
United Kingdom	514	
Poland	526	
Ireland	522	
Liechtenstein	525	
Slovenia	514	
Switzerland	515	
Belgium	505	
OECD average	501	
Chinese Taipei	523	
Luxembourg	491	
Viet Nam	528	
France	499	
Austria	506	
Czech Republic	508	
Norway	495	
United States	497	
Denmark	498	
Macao-China	521	
Sweden	485	
Italy	494	
Hungary	494	
Israel	470	
Iceland	478	
Lithuania	496